THE OLD CASTLE OF KILKERRAN

(Pen and wash drawing by John Wilson, R.A., 1813)

FERGUSSON

Ferguson

Atholl was the early home of this Clan, where it was established before the reign of Bruce, having come there from its original lands of Strachur in Argyll.

The Fergusons joined the Athollmen who fought with Montrose and their kinsmen of Atholl and Strathardle fought in The '45 for Prince Charles.

The Lands of Balquhidder have been in Ferguson hands for some six hundred years and in Aberdeenshire they have owned estates for four centuries.

Annie Laurie of Maxwelton, famed in song the world over, became the wife of Ferguson of Craigdarroch.

Badge—**Pine (Strachur) & Poplar (Atholl).**

For a small charge to cover research, information on your Tartan connection and/or Highland dress may be obtained from The Scottish Tartans Society, Comrie, Perthshire, Scotland. (Registered Charity.) July, 1975.

THE FERGUSSONS

Their Lowland and Highland Branches

BY

SIR JAMES FERGUSSON
OF KILKERRAN, BARONET

Cheif of the Name
Formerly Keeper of the Records of Scotland

"We have our good service to plead for us, and that
we have been honest and loyal from the beginning, and
will continue so to the end."—Major-General JAMES
FERGUSON OF BALMAKELLY (*d.* 1705).

With Tartan and Arms in Colour, and a Map

JOHNSTON & BACON
EDINBURGH AND LONDON

First published 1956
Reprinted 1970
Reprinted 1973

© *Johnston & Bacon Publishers*

SBN 7179 4522 7

PRINTED IN GREAT BRITAIN BY
LOWE AND BRYDONE (PRINTERS) LTD., THETFORD, NORFOLK

Preface

In framing this brief account of the Fergussons, I have profited gratefully from the labours of our two historians, James Ferguson and the Rev. Robert Menzies Fergusson, who under the auspices of the Clan Fergus(s)on Society published *Records of the Clan and Name of Fergusson, Ferguson, and Fergus* in 1895 and a *Supplement* thereto in 1899. These two volumes have become very rare, but can be consulted in any public library. They contain a mass of very accurate information, as well as a fair seasoning of such traditions and legends connected with the name as could be gathered at the close of last century.

Statements in the following pages for which no footnote references are given are mostly taken from the *Records*, but I have checked and supplemented them where possible.

J. F.

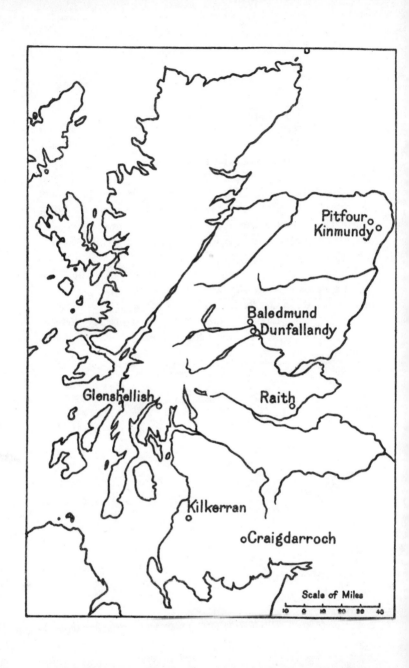

Pitfour
Kinmundy

Baledmund
Dunfallandy

Glenshellish

Raith

Kilkerran

Craigdarroch

Scale of Miles

10   0   10   20   30   40

The Fergussons

THE name of Fergusson or Ferguson has long been widely
spread in . Scotland, from Ross-shire to Dumfriesshire
and from Fife to Argyll and even St. Kilda, as well as
among Scottish emigrants and settlers in other countries.
Why its distribution in Scotland should be so scattered is
hard to say. History can explain how Gordons migrated
from Berwickshire to Moray, or Balfours from Fife to
Orkney. But though there are traditions, probably of
no great age, purporting to explain the wide dispersal of
the Fergussons, and why families of the name with similar
armorial bearings are found in Ayrshire, Atholl, and
Aberdeenshire, there is no real evidence. All we know
for certain is that when the sound, impartial testimony
of contemporary records begins, in the thirteenth century,
there were men in widely separated districts of Scotland
who alike called themselves sons of Fergus.

By the middle of the fifteenth century, when surnames
had become usual and from which record evidence is
more plentiful, the Fergussons of Craigdarroch in
Dumfriesshire, of Kilkerran and Auchinsoull in Ayrshire,
and of Derculich or Dunfallandy in Perthshire were all
well established as landed families, and had obviously
been so for some generations. Other families whose
origin, for lack of written evidence, is unknown may be
nearly as old. The name also occurs quite early in the
burghs, and by the time of the Union of the Crowns it
was common in Inverurie, Aberdeen, Dundee, Perth,

Dunfermline, Inverkeithing, Stirling, Edinburgh, Ayr, Dumfries, Lochmaben, and elsewhere. Five bearers of it have been provosts of Ayr.

FORMS OF THE NAME

The name is, of course, originally a Gaelic patronymic —MacFhearghuis. By the time of James VI it had been widely anglicised as Fergus-son. Fergushill or Fergussill was an Ayrshire variant of the name, now very rare or extinct. David Fergushill, provost of Ayr between 1596 and 1607, is on record variously as Fergushill and Fergussoun, and his family probably assimilated their name to that of the much more numerous Fergussons. The original Gaelic form became corrupted in writing into such widely different forms as MacFergus, Mac-Ferries, and MacFirries ; or, since the aspirated f and g are both silent in Gaelic, into MacErries, MacHerries, MacKerras (a form once common in Argyll and known to-day in Australia), and even MacIrish. Or the prefix was dropped altogether and the name remained Fergus, Fergie, Ferrie, and Ferries.[1] Such corruptions are not unusual. Other Gaelic names show the same double line of descent and corruption. MacAlasdair, for example, retains the same sound in many spellings, or becomes in its anglicised form MacAlexander, Alexander, Sanderson, and Sanders.

The shortened form of the name with the single " s " was adopted by record clerks before 1600, but I have not found any bearer of the name signing himself in that form before the eighteenth century. About 1600 the commonest spelling was Fergussoun, and in Charles II's time Fergussone. But spelling in the old days was a

[1] These and yet other variations are listed in George F. Black's *The Surnames of Scotland*. One found in S.W. Scotland is Forgie.

matter of individual choice. One Fergusson of Kilkerran signed himself in 1518 as " Forgisson," and another wrote his name in three different ways at different periods of his life.

In modern, times the families of Ayrshire, Dumfriesshire, Argyll, and Perthshire have generally retained the double " s," and those of Aberdeenshire, Fife, Angus, and in Ireland have used the single one, which has also been generally adopted by those settling in the cities. The difference is of little significance, except that the shortened form somewhat obscures the patronymic origin.

ORIGINS OF THE NAME

It is generally alleged that all Fergussons claim descent from Fergus Mor mac Erc, a very early king of the Scots in Argyll of whom his bare existence is about the only fact known.[1] But though this tradition was probably held by the Fergussons living in the central and western Highlands, there may well have been other eponymous ancestors. In particular there is some evidence strongly suggesting that the south-western Fergussons, living in Ayrshire and Dumfriesshire, took their name from Fergus, Prince of Galloway, a much less shadowy personage, who was an important figure in the reigns of David I and Malcolm IV. He restored the see of Whithorn, founded the Abbey of Dundrennan, and died, as a monk of Holyrood, in 1161. This prince was the grandfather of Duncan, first Earl of Carrick, who was in turn the great-grandfather of King Robert Bruce, through whom that title passed into our Royal family. The first Earl of Carrick seems to have made a point of styling himself in his charters " Duncan, son of Gilbert

---

[1] A. O. Anderson : *The Early Sources of Scottish History*, pp. cxviii, cxxix, cxliii.

the son of Fergus," [1] and this suggests the beginning of the use of " Fergus-son " as a surname.

CLAN AND CHIEF

It is improbable that the Fergussons had any single common origin. As far back as we can find enough evidence on which to base theories, we notice at least five main groups of Fergussons existing independently—two in the south-west, one in Argyll, one in north-eastern Perthshire and Angus, and one in Aberdeenshire—not to mention others in Balquhidder and Strathyre, in Fife, and in Ross-shire. These groups were so widely separated that they never could and, in fact, never did regard themselves as one clan in the same sense as, for example, the Campbells, Macdonalds and Macleans of the Isles, Macleods, Grants, or Munros.

A clan, as regarded by the King, the Privy Council, and Parliament in the sixteenth and seventeenth centuries, was a group of families and their adherents occupying a defined region either in the Highlands or along the English Border, many of them—but by no means all—claiming descent from a common ancestor, and all owning allegiance to one chief (who was not necessarily their landlord), and expressing it by submitting to his jurisdiction in peace and rising at his summons to follow him in war. A clan included many who did not bear the same name as the chief and his relatives.

Applying these standards, we can trace at least three and perhaps four groups of Fergussons who lived in the style of a clan under their respective chiefs before the eighteenth century. An account of each is given below.

The authority of a chief was often reinforced and

---

[1] *Liber Sancte Marie de Melros*, i. pp. 20, 22, 25 ; *Chronica*, ed. Stubbs, Rolls Series, iv. p. 145.

DULCIUS·EX·ASPERIS

UT·PROSIM·ALIIS

PERSONAL ARMS OF FERGUSSON OF KILKERRAN

PERSONAL ARMS OF FERGUSSON OF DUNFALLANDY

PERSONAL ARMS OF FERGUSSON OF CRAIGDARROCH

legally supported, from the time of King Robert Bruce onwards, by a grant from the Crown of a barony. This was the lowest of the feudal jurisdictions by means of which the Sovereign devolved and decentralised the responsibility for maintaining peace and order, administering justice, and raising the royal revenue. A baron was not a peer, although down to 1587 he had the right to sit in Parliament : after that date the barons elected their representatives, who formed, down to the Union of the Parliaments, one of the Three Estates. A baron was a landowner who not only held his lands direct from the King or from the Prince of Scotland, but had been granted by the King the right to hold a court of justice on his lands. A barony, in short, was not an estate but a jurisdiction. In the baron court not only were rents collected but minor crimes and misdemeanours could be tried and punished by fine or imprisonment, debtors could be pursued, and decrees could be issued " with consent of the laird and the haill tenants " like acts of a little Parliament, to promote good husbandry, neighbourly behaviour, and the general welfare of the countryside. Down to 1747 and even after it, the barony was an important social and administrative unit, and certain legal rights attach to it to this day.

Kilkerran was a barony before the fifteenth century, but the baronial rights were forfeited ;[1] they were restored in 1701 when the lands were of new erected into a barony by charter from King William. Baledmund and Kinmundy were also baronies. Fergusson of Dun-

---

[1] They were resumed by James IV " on account of the alienation of the lands or of the greater part of them without the superior's consent " (*Register of the Great Seal*, ii. 3696 ; iii. 2268) ; but Kilkerran is still described as a barony in conveyances of 1604, 1625, and 1659 (Secretary's Register of Sasines, Ayr, ii. f. 328 ; P.R. Sasines, Ayr, iii. f. 228, ix. f. 423) ; and an *ad hoc* meeting of the Baron Court of Kilkerran was held on 16 October 1693 (minute in Kilkerran MSS.).

fallandy was, as will be explained later, often referred to as a baron, and so was Fergusson of Muling, but Dunfallandy and Muling never in fact had charters of barony. Neither had Craigdarroch ; but since the family of Fergusson of Craigdarroch in Dumfriesshire has the longest recorded history of any landed family of Fergussons a summary of it may be given precedence.

FERGUSSON OF CRAIGDARROCH

The oldest charter of this family, granting lands in Glencairn to a Fergusson of Craigdarroch, is undated but belongs to the reign of David II (1329–71). Another is of 1398, and a third of 1484. Since others are missing, the descent of the family is not clear before 1454, but thereafter it can be traced directly to modern times. Several of its members were members of Parliament both before and after the Union. The line ended in an heiress who married in 1918 Colonel Wallace Smith-Cuninghame of Caprington, and the old estate has been sold ; but one of her sons, Mr. John Fergusson-Cuninghame, still owns some of the superiorities of the family lands.

Craigdarroch's principal branches were the Fergussons of Isle and the Fergussons of Caitloch, traceable from the late sixteenth and early seventeenth century respectively but both now extinct ; others were the Fergussons of Chapelmark, their descendants the Fergussons of Corrochdow, on record in the early 1600's, and the Fergussons of Fourmerkland. The Fergussons of Spitalhaugh in Peeblesshire, who came from Lochmaben, were probably another branch of this famous stock.

Craigdarroch is a dignified eighteenth-century house in the parish of Glencairn, not far from Moniaive. The tower of Isle, built by John Fergusson of Isle in 1585, is about five miles from Dumfries and of considerable architectural interest, besides still retaining its iron " yett."

The Dumfriesshire Fergussons were more law-abiding than some Border clans and were occasionally summoned by the King to join a muster of the royal forces against them. In the seventeenth century they were nearly all staunch Covenanters. The signatures of William Fergusson of Craigdarroch and John Fergusson of Corrochdow to the National Covenant of 1638 are both extant. Robert Fergusson of Craigdarroch at the head of a troop of Nithsdale men had a victorious skirmish with a party of Cromwell's cavalry. John Fergusson of Craigdarroch was killed fighting under Mackay at Killiecrankie in 1689, and the saddle on which he rode that day is still preserved by his descendants. William Fergusson of Caitloch was prominent among the Covenant leaders at the battle of Bothwell Brig in 1679. But the Caitloch family, though their sufferings under Charles II and James VII gave them no cause to love the Stewarts, subsequently turned Jacobite, and a daughter of this house was the wife of the execrated John Murray of Broughton. James Fergusson of Craigdarroch, on the other hand, who was Chamberlain to the Duke of Queensberry, was in 1745 a most active supporter of the Government and the Protestant succession.

Two eighteenth-century members of the Craigdarroch family have achieved a fortuitous fame in verse. Anna Laurie (died in 1764), daughter of Sir Robert Laurie of Maxwelton and wife of Alexander Fergusson of Craigdarroch, is the heroine of Lady John Scott's famous song " Annie Laurie " ; and her grandson, another Alexander, won the Bacchanalian contest celebrated by Burns in " The Whistle."

FERGUSSON OF DUNFALLANDY

The Dunfallandy family, with its many branches of which the Fergussons of Muling, Ballyoukan, Balmacruchie, Baledmund, and Middlehaugh were the principal, was influential over a wide stretch of Perthshire from the banks of the Tummel north-eastwards to Strathardle and Glenshee. It can be traced from before 1489 under the name of Fergusson of Derculich, but from about 1620 onwards, having parted with the Derculich lands, it is known as " of Dunfallandy."

Various heads of this family were colloquially designated " Baron Fergusson " from as early as 1585 right down to 1746, although, as already stated, the lands were not in fact a barony. The nickname shows what influence the Dunfallandy chieftains were supposed to wield. That it was only a nickname is clear from the form of its appearance in various official records, for instance " Johnne Fergusone of Darcloch *alias* Barroun Fergussone " in 1585 and " Johne Fergussoun called Barone Fergussone " in 1607.[1]

The Atholl Fergussons, like most of the clans in the central Highlands, were a constant trouble to the King's government, and their lands often provided a refuge for the " broken men," the wandering bandits, especially the turbulent and proscribed Macgregors, for whose misbehaviour no chief liked to accept responsibility. The " Fergussonis " are listed among the Atholl clans on the roll, drawn up in 1585, of those clans " that hes capitanis, cheiffis, and chiftennis quhomeon they depend, oftymes aganis the willis of thair landislordis, alsweill on the Bordouris as Hielandis." [2] Not surprisingly, " Baron

[1] *Register of the Privy Council*, iv. p. 813 ; vii. p. 685 ; xiv. p. 533.
[2] *Acts of the Parliament of Scotland*, iii. p. 467.

Fergusoun" of Dunfallandy was one of the landed proprietors ordered to find caution in that same year for the good conduct of those living on his lands, under the Act of Parliament " for the quieting and keping in obedience of the disorderit subjectis inhabitantis of the Bordouris, Hielandis, and Ilis " ; [1] but it was not till 1591 that he reluctantly consented to do so, and his guarantee cannot have been effective for he was again called upon, with several other chieftains, in 1607.[2]

Another Fergusson chieftain in Atholl, David Fergusson of Muling, seems to have made no effort whatever to control his people, and was himself not sufficiently civilised to be able to write his own name.[3] Various of his dependents were accused of assault, robbery, and a particularly brutal murder committed in 1597, and he himself was in 1602 denounced rebel for not appearing when summoned to answer for them.[4] Muling, by the way, was not in the parish of Moulin but in part of Redgorton which is now in Logiealmond.

The family of Fergusson of Baledmund, still flourishing, was founded by one Finlay Fergusson who first appears on record in 1602,[5] and who received a charter of lands from Sir Archibald Stewart of Fynnart in 1612.

In Strathyre and Balquhidder the Fergussons have been long established and are still numerous, but as there were no landed proprietors among them their history is not well documented. They do not seem to have owed allegiance to any chief, and were, like their kinsmen in Atholl and their neighbours the Macgregors and Maclarens, a constant trouble to the authorities.

[1] *Ibid.*, pp. 461–5.
[2] *Register of the Privy Council*, iv. pp. 803, 813 ; xiv. p. 533.
[3] He signed documents by a notary ; see Register of Deeds, ciii. ff. 233–4, and cp. several entries in vol. civ.
[4] *Register of the Privy Council*, vi. pp. 414–5, 486.
[5] Register of Deeds, ciii. f. 196.

A certain Duncan Fergusson in Strathyre was one of several men accused in 1612 of killing the King's deer in the Forest of Glenfinglas with " hagbuts, bowis, and utheris ingynis," and denounced as rebels on their non-appearance.[1]

By the end of the eighteenth century, however, the people living in Balquhidder and along Lochearnside were described as " modest, peaceable, and very obliging . . . lively, intelligent, fond of news, and hospitable to strangers." A minister of Comrie made the curious observation that, of the diseases prevalent in the neighbourhood, " colics have sometimes proved fatal, particularly (it is remarked) to those of the name of *Fergusson.*" [2]

A young man living at Easter Auchraw on Lochearnside at that time grew up to be a famous mason and master-builder. He was Robert Fergusson, called " *Rob-a-Clachair* " (" Rob the Mason "), and belonged to a family of masons whose representatives were still numerous in Balquhidder fifty years ago. *Rob-a-Clachair* was the builder, and perhaps the designer, of the mansion house of Ardvorlich, and of Lochiel's house of Achnacarry. He also had a great local reputation as an amateur bonesetter.

Of the principal Fergusson houses in Perthshire, Dunfallandy itself and Baledmund are still in the possession of the old families, and still occupied and maintained. The old house of Dunfallandy was destroyed by a fire, but was very handsomely rebuilt in the traditional style in 1818.

Like several other warlike Highland families, the Perthshire Fergussons developed a Jacobite tradition. Many of them probably fought under Montrose. A generation later some of them joined after Killiecrankie

[1] *Register of the Privy Council,* ix: p. 457.
[2] *Statistical Account of Scotland,* vi. p. 97 ; xi. pp. 179, 186. .

the Highland army which the Viscount of Dundee had commanded and which was beaten back in disorder a week or two later by the Cameronian regiment at Dunkeld. Finlay Fergusson of Baledmund was out, apparently against his will, in the 'Fifteen, and John Fergusson of Dunfallandy and Thomas Fergusson of Ballyoukan in the 'Forty-five. Dunfallandy was taken prisoner, and was fortunate to escape condemnation when he was tried at Carlisle in the summer of 1746. Some of the Strathardle Fergussons are also said to have been out in the 'Forty-five.

The Fergussons as a whole, however, cannot be rated as one of the Jacobite clans. Of the Jacobite prisoners whose records have been published, numbering no less than 3,471, only twenty-one were named Fergusson, Ferguson, or, in one case, McFairish (MacFhearghuis). Almost all these belonged to Perthshire, and seven of them are recorded to have served in the Duke of Perth's regiment.[1] Many of the Argyll Fergussons, on the other hand, served in the Argyll militia which garrisoned the forts and castles of the West Highlands for King George, and some of them fought, not without distinction, at Falkirk and Culloden ; while members of the Kilkerran, Craigdarroch, and Kinmundy families were in various ways active on the Government side. Kinmundy House in Aberdeenshire, built in 1736, was looted by the Jacobites and narrowly escaped being burnt. Thomas Fergusson of Ballyoukan was wounded at Culloden on the Jacobite side, but on the Government side another cadet of Dunfallandy, Captain Thomas Fergusson, adjutant of the Buffs, killed a Highlander by cutting off his head with a single blow.

It is not surprising that the Argyll and Lowland

[1] Sir Bruce Seton and Jean Arnot : *The Prisoners of the '45*, ii. pp. 186–90 ; iii. p. 86.

Fergussons should at that time have been on the opposite side to those of their name from the central Highlands. Indeed their separation illustrates the general division of Scotland in the 'Forty-five. Five-sixths of Prince Charles Edward's army was Highland, and it had practically no support from the Lowlands, except in the north-east, or from Argyll.

FERGUSSON OF KILKERRAN

The Kilkerran Fergussons first appear on record in the 15th century. John Fergusson of Kilkerran, recorded in 1464, was probably the son of Duncan, son of Colin, "*dominus de Kylkerane*," on record in 1439. They may have been descended from a "John son of Fergus" who was one of the witnesses to a charter by Edward Bruce signed at Turnberry shortly after Bannockburn.[1]

At the beginning of James II's reign there were two prominent and related families of Fergussons in Carrick, one living at Auchinsoull on the Stinchar and the other at Kilkerran near the Girvan : Auchinsoull was possibly the elder, but never claimed to be the principal—it died out some 150 years ago. The Fergussons of Knockgerran, who held land of the abbot and convent of Crossraguel from before 1485 till 1527, were probably a branch of the Kilkerran family.

By 1600 there were Fergussons all over the southern part of Carrick, their homes scattered up and down the Girvan and Stinchar valleys and between them, as far north as Maybole (besides several in Ayr) and as far south as the borders of Galloway. All these owned Kilkerran as their chief. In the great Carrick feud between the rival Kennedy families of Cassillis and Bargany, the Fergussons, although they lived nearer to

---

[1] *National MSS. of Scotland*, ii. No. XXIII.

Bargany, sided with the Earl of Cassillis. "Bernard Fergussone and all his," writes a contemporary, "hes bene and ar frendis and dependentis on the houss of Cassillis."[1] Some Fergussons were in the Earl of Cassillis's party in the fight just outside Maybole on the dark winter day of 1601 when the laird of Bargany met his death.

A generation earlier the Fergussons had had a feud of their own with the Craufurds of Camlarg, which created enough disturbance in Carrick to attract the notice of the Privy Council in 1564.[2] It seems to have arisen out of the irregular occupation by the Craufurds of some farms on the sea-coast south of Girvan belonging to Bernard Fergusson of Kilkerran, then a young man. Its culminating incident took place in Ayr on 31 July 1564 when he rode in with more than a hundred men, including two of his brothers and his kinsmen Fergusson of Dalduff and Fergusson of Threave, and entered the Tolbooth of Ayr where the Sheriff Court was sitting and John Craufurd of Camlarg was present. The Fergussons, "efter injurious wordis,"[3] attacked the Craufurds with drawn swords, "and thairthrow trublit the said court and stoppit the said scheref deputis to minister justice." No one seems to have been killed; but Kilkerran and his principal adherents were summoned to appear before the Court of Justiciary in Edinburgh and punished by a fine.[4]

---

[1] *Correspondence of Sir Patrick Waus of Barnbarroch*, p. 126.

[2] *Calendar of Scottish Papers*, ii. pp. 76–7.

[3] The words are not recorded, as they are in a case of assault of 1610. On that occasion David Fergushill, an elderly man who had been till lately provost of Ayr, was attacked at the mercat cross by one of the bailies of the burgh named David Craufurd, who, "without regaird had be him to the dewtifull cariage and modest behaviour of a civile magistrat . . . oppinlie and publictlie out of his unrewlie and distemperat humour, efter a most bitter and scornfull maner, first cryit him 'Bo, carle! Bo, carle!' . . ." —*Register of the Privy Council: Acta*, 1609–10, ff. 39–40.

[4] Pitcairn's *Criminal Trials in Scotland*, i. pp. 456–7.

In the seventeenth century the Fergussons of Carrick were nearly all Covenanters like other Ayrshiremen, with the rather strange exception of Sir John Fergusson of Kilkerran (who was knighted by Charles I about 1641) and his four sons—a quarrelsome generation, often at odds with their neighbours—one of whom served in 1648 in the ill-fated Royalist army of " the Engagement " which was scattered by Cromwell at Preston. In general, Ayrshire was a stronghold of the Covenant, and loyalty to the Protestant succession at and after the Revolution was so deep that in 1746 the county was reputed not to have produced a single rebel in the last Jacobite rising.

Sir John Fergusson of Kilkerran, who died in 1647, left his property heavily encumbered with debts, and by the time of his grandson Alexander almost the whole of the family estate was held in pledge by a neighbour who had acquired the various bonds over it—John, 2nd Lord Bargany. Another of Sir John's grandsons, however, cleared off the debts and recovered the lands. The Kilkerran family descended from him has produced four Members of Parliament, two Lords of Session, a General, and an Admiral.

In the two centuries between the Reformation and the accession of George III there were several landed families of Fergussons in Carrick, all cadets of Kilkerran— Auchinsoull, Threave, Dalduff, Letterpin, Millenderdaill, Finnart, and others—but all these have been long extinct, though the name is still common in Ayrshire. The Kilkerran family alone remained on their ancestral lands, and John Fergusson of Kilkerran, the recoverer of its fortunes, who was created a baronet in 1703, was granted in 1719 the undifferenced arms which denote the chief of the name. His son and grandson, both lawyers like him, were notable agricultural improvers, and the present landscape of the middle Girvan valley is largely their creation.

The old house of Kilkerran, a strong, lofty tower built probably in the fifteenth century, has long been a ruin, its name having been transferred to another old house two miles away which Sir John acquired in 1686 and rebuilt about 1695. This, enlarged in 1814, is still the family home. Threave still stands, though much altered ; the other old places named have been rebuilt as farmhouses, except Finnart on Loch Ryan, which was pulled down a few years ago by an unappreciative purchaser.

FERGUSSONS IN ARGYLL

In the Cowal and Kintyre districts of Argyll, the name of Fergusson is of immemorial antiquity, often recorded in the nearly Gaelic form of McKerras. But little is recorded of the name in early times except that the Cowal Fergussons gave a bond of manrent to the Earl of Argyll in 1568. (Curle MSS in Register House.)

The principal Fergusson family there, however, had an interesting history. The lands of Glenshellish, near the head of Loch Eck, were held of the Earls (later Dukes) of Argyll for at least 200 years, and probably longer, by a family sometimes styled McKerras and subsequently Fergusson. The last of the family to possess these lands was Daniel Fergusson of Glenshellish who died early in 1803. Having fallen deeply into debt, chiefly through his eldest son John's being, as the unfortunate father observed, " of a very improvident disposition," he was obliged to sell Glenshellish in 1801. The estate fetched £6,430, which Daniel Fergusson assigned to trustees for the benefit of his wife, Christian Fletcher, and his other sons about a year before his own death.[1]

[1] Register of Deeds (Durie), vol. 297, pp. 198–201 ; vol. 298, pp. 109–10.

The head of this family possessed heritably along with the Glenshellish lands the office of " serjeant or mair of fee " of the lands of Strachur under the Earl of Argyll as Bailie of Cowal, and used to receive a wand of office along with the customary earth and stone when he took sasine of the lands.[1] The arms of the last representative of the family—Seumas, styled Chief of Clannfhearghuis of Stra-chur, an adventurous traveller who latterly lived in New York—bore this wand as a mark of difference, in appropriate commemoration of this ancient office. This family is now extinct.

FERGUSONS IN ABERDEENSHIRE AND FIFE

In the east and north-east of Scotland there have been several families of the name, some of considerable antiquity. In Aberdeenshire we find some variants of the usual form of the name. A Katherine Ferries or McFerries was accused of witchcraft in Aberdeen in 1597. Two Deeside ministers in the seventeenth century called themselves sometimes Ferries and sometimes Ferguson. And the Fergusons of Badifurrow, who acquired that estate in 1655, were descended from a burgess family of Inverurie who can be traced back to 1553 and who down to 1610 if not later were always called Fergus.[2]

Badifurrow had by the eighteenth century no less than seven flourishing branches ; and some of its cadets, pursuing their fortunes overseas in the traditional manner of Scottish younger sons, rose to distinction in various countries of Europe. Those branches which lasted longest were Kinmundy, already mentioned, and the distinguished house of Pitfour.

[1] *The Argyll Sasines*, ed. Herbert Campbell, i. Nos. 50, 455–6.
[2] *Register of the Privy Seal*, iv. 2090–1 ; *Register of the Privy Council*, v. p. 631 ; viii. p. 732 ; ix. p. 22 ; xi. p. 64.

The name is well spread in Fife and Angus, and has had a long continuance in the burgh of Dundee—whence came David Fergusson the Reformer, one of the earliest Moderators of the General Assembly—in Dunfermline (where a Michael " Fargisone " was admitted a burgess in 1499), in Kirkcaldy, and in Inverkeithing. It was from a burgess family established in Inverkeithing for some two centuries that the family of Ferguson (now Munro-Ferguson) of Raith arose, which has produced some eminent soldiers and statesmen.

OTHER FERGUSONS

In the west, there was a family of merchants and craftsmen of the name of Fergus in the burgh of Kirkintilloch for some generations during the eighteenth and early nineteenth centuries. With the growth of Glasgow into the biggest city of Scotland, Fergussons and Fergusons have become numerous there ; most of them, no doubt, are the posterity of incomers from Argyll, Ayrshire, Stirlingshire, Strathyre, and Balquhidder, but the name goes back to 1422 in the city's records, and is probably as old in Edinburgh.

There have been several landed families of Fergusons in Ulster, some of whom claim to have migrated from Ayrshire, and may well have settled there as part of James VI's Plantation of that province, or have fled there during the troubled years of Charles II's and James VII's reigns. Some, however, may be of original native stock.

For centuries, too, families of the name have been established in the Netherlands, where many Fergusons served in the famous Scots Brigade, the most distinguished regiment in the service of the United Provinces, whose boast was that they had never lost a stand of colours in battle ; also in Germany, in Poland, and in Russia. The name flourishes to-day, too, throughout the Commonwealth, especially in Canada, and in the United States.

THE CHIEF

As has already been pointed out, in the old days when clans were recognised social groups, named as such in statutes, official minutes, and commissions of justiciary, the various families of Fergussons were never regarded, nor regarded themselves, as one clan ; and no one laird or baron was held responsible by the Government for the conduct of all the Fergussons in Scotland or even all the Fergussons in the Highlands.

But when the country grew more peaceful with the firmer establishment of a central authority, and after the old feudal jurisdictions were either done away with or (in the case of the baron courts) stringently reduced, there came a change in the conception of a clan. Clanship grew less real in the old sense of an intertwining of land tenure and military service, but became stronger in the sentiment of kinship between all bearers of the same name. The local loyalty weakened, but the nation-wide loyalty was augmented. The growth of this modern clan feeling may be ascribed in great measure to the writings of Sir Walter Scott, who, if he did not understand much about Highland clans, certainly knew a very great deal about the Border ones ; and his genius created in the minds of the Scottish people something which, if not of wholly legitimate historical descent, has nevertheless proved itself strong and enduring.

This vitality of the clan spirit is expressed by the growth in recent years of numerous clan societies designed for social intercourse between bearers of ancient and historic names and for preserving their traditions. The present enormous interest in Scottish genealogy is a further illustration of it. And there could be no doubt at the first meetings in Glasgow in 1954 of the revived Clan Fergus(s)on Society of the warm desire of those assembled to associate themselves in an active body expressive of the traditions of the name they bore.

Another important factor in maintaining clan feeling has been the stricter interpretation and administration of the law of heraldry by successive holders of the office of Lord Lyon King of Arms. An Act of Parliament of 1672 ensures that no arms are recognised except those entered in the Public Register, and the rights of individual holders of arms are carefully protected. Since 1672 no one has been allowed to assume the arms of the head of a family except their rightful owner who has registered them and paid the statutory fees. Hence legal recognition defines the head of every clan, family, and cadet branch, each of whom can be known by the armorial bearings which are peculiarly his.

It is during the eighteenth century that various incidents are to be noted showing that the head of the Kilkerran family came gradually to be regarded as chief of the whole name of Fergusson. The legal recognition came first. Sir John Fergusson of Kilkerran, 1st baronet, baron of Kilkerran and Barclanachan, was granted the undifferenced arms of Fergusson by the Lord Lyon of that time, Sir Charles Erskine of Cambo, a sound herald and genealogist, in 1719. In 1727 the heads of the Aberdeenshire families of Fergusson of Kinmundy and Ferguson of Pitfour appealed to Sir John's successor, Sir James Fergusson, 2nd baronet, then a rising advocate and later a judge, to settle a dispute between them. In 1753 Sir James (by then styled Lord Kilkerran) was granted a Royal warrant to add supporters to his arms, as are regularly borne by chiefs. A generation later

Robert Fergusson the poet, who came of an Aberdeen-shire family, presented a copy of his book of poems to Sir Adam Fergusson of Kilkerran ; and a Strachur Fergusson had the arms of " the Honourable Fergussons of Kilcarran " carved on his family tombstone, which is to be seen to this day in the kirkyard of Strachur. It is striking also that in 1788 a poor Highland minister in Benbecula, the Rev. Duncan Ferguson, anxious to get a charge in a mainland parish, appealed for help not to one of the local chiefs or landowners but to Sir Adam, far away in Ayrshire, the chief of his name.

Fergusson of Dunfallandy and Fergusson of Stra-chur have both in recent years been permitted by the Lord Lyon to add supporters to their arms, as chieftains, but Stra-chur, as already noted, left no heir.

CONCLUSION

After the eighteenth century, the history of the Fergussons can no longer be traced through large territorial groups, and the only continuity is through individual families. Since 1800 the whole balance of Scottish population has changed, so that we are now a predominantly urban and industrial people, and there are many more Fergussons and Fergusons, like bearers of other names, in the cities and towns than in the country.

Yet by far the greater part of these town-dwellers are countrymen by descent, not more than three or four generations removed from the Braes of Balquhidder, the wooded valleys of Carrick, the fields and farms of the north-east, or the hills above Loch Fyne ; and none should forget the rock whence he was hewn. The traditions of any clan can be maintained only if there survives a pride in the native soil of its growth and in the principal families from which are descended many more clansmen than they themselves perhaps realise.

A clan is, above all, the ideal of a great family. This family of the sons of Fergus has bred sons who have rendered honourable service to Scotland, to Great Britain, and to the British Commonwealth, as soldiers, sailors, ministers, statesmen, administrators, lawyers, physicians, scientists, and men of letters. Their achievements have given a lustre to their name in which every bearer of it can feel a pride and find an example.

Appendix I

THE armorial bearings of the various families of the name are of two classes : those which show as the principal figures *Azure, a buckle argent between three boars' heads couped or*, and those which show *Argent, a lion rampant azure*, with subordinate charges on a chief of which the tincture varies. The first are borne by the Ayrshire, Aberdeenshire, Argyll and Perthshire families, and the second by those of Dumfriesshire and Fife. Both have been much diversified with distinguishing marks. Crests have varied even more, and have included a bee on a thistle, a hand grasping a broken spear, a crescent (sometimes by itself and sometimes issuing from a cloud), a demi-lion, and other devices. Of the several Fergusson mottos, the one most generally borne is *Dulcius ex asperis* (" Sweeter from difficulties ") in allusion to the bee's labours in winning honey from the thistle.

The Act of 1672, " Concerning the Priviledges of the Office of Lyon King of Arms," which is still in force, obliges all bearers of arms to register them, and provides penalties of fine and escheat for misusing them. The Lyon is also empowered to grant new arms to " vertuous and well deserving persons," with suitable differences and marks of cadency. The Register enables authorised arms to be traced back for over 300 years. The arms of Fergusson of Craigdarroch were first registered in 1673, Ferguson of Kinmundy in 1691, Fergusson of Kilkerran in 1719, Ferguson of Raith in 1725, Fergusson of Pitfour in 1734, and Fergusson of Isle in 1788. The arms of Ferguson-Tepper, the Polish descendant of Badifurrow, were registered in the College of Arms in London in 1779.

Many of these coats, however, are of far older date than 1672. What is now the coat of Fergusson of Kilkerran is found in two heraldic manuscripts of the beginning of the seventeenth century. It is not, however, the original one, for the seal of Duncan Fergusson of Kilkerran in 1518 bore a chevron with a mullet above it and a cross-crosslet below ; and this seems to record a tradition of a descent from Fergus, Prince of Galloway, for the Earls of Carrick descended from him bore a chevron on their shield, and the Earls of Cassillis, of similar descent, a chevron between three cross-crosslets. The arms of the Craigdarroch Fergussons seem to point to a descent from this Fergus likewise, for the lion rampant, their principal figure, was the armorial device of Alan, Lord of Galloway, Fergus's grandson.

All arms are *personal* , and by registration and payment of the statutory fees become the personal and heritable property of the bearer. But the right to bear arms is by no means restricted to chiefs and heads of families, for all " vertuous and well deserving persons " may apply to Lyon for a grant of arms suitably devised and differenced. Anyone, too, may use the arms or crest of his chief provided he so displays them as to express his allegiance to the owner of the arms, either by subjoining such words as

" The arms of the Chief " or by surrounding the device with a strap and buckle, symbolising the wearing of it on arm or breast, as the chief's followers used to do, either in battles or in peaceful gatherings, to distinguish each other and show their common loyalty.

This is the only way in which one person can legally display the arms of another. Despite the commercial exploitation of arms and crests in the souvenir shops to beguile ignorant tourists, there are properly no such things as " clan arms " or " clan crests."

The plant badge of the Fergussons is generally stated to be the little sunflower or rock-rose, and the Atholl Fergussons are also said to have worn the bog-myrtle. But the Lyon's ruling is that the badge of the Kilkerran and Dunfallandy families is the poplar, and that of Fergusson of Strachur the pine. The poplar is the aspen (*populus tremulans*).

Appendix II

SOME DISTINGUISHED BEARERS OF THE NAME

Mr. DAVID FERGUSSON (*c.* 1525–98), one of the leading Reformers of the Church of Scotland, appointed minister of Dunfermline in 1560, and elected Moderator of the General Assembly in 1573 and again in 1578. He has been described as " one of the boldest, most sagacious, and most amiable of the Reformers," and had much influence both with other Church leaders and with King James VI. Noted for witty and pithy sayings (it was he who coined the term " tulchan Bishops "), he made a collection of Scottish proverbs, the first of its kind, which was published in 1641. At his death he was the father of the Church, " the auldest minister that tyme in Scotland." There is a small portrait of him at Kilkerran.

WILLIAM GOUW FERGUSON (c. 1633–c.1690), a still-life painter of the Dutch school, examples of whose work are in many public art galleries. He is said to have studied in Scotland before going to the Continent, but his ancestry is not known.

Maj.-Gen. JAMES FERGUSON OF BALMAKELLY (died 1705), ancestor of the Fergusons of Kinmundy, was the third son of William Ferguson of Badifurrow. When very young he joined the Scots Brigade in the Netherlands service. By 1688 he was a captain, and came over to England with William of Orange. He served at Killiecrankie, and after it, promoted major, commanded the expedition to the West Highlands which began the construction of Fort William, and defeated the Jacobites in Mull. He fought at Steenkirk in 1692, and was then promoted to command the Cameronian regiment. He was prominent in Marlborough's attack on the Schellenberg, and commanded a brigade at Blenheim. In 1705, when he had just become a Major-General, he died suddenly at Bois-le-Duc, when Marlborough was about to leave him in command of the army. " All the English themselves," wrote one of his officers, " allowed he was by much the best officer we had in all the British troops. He was brave, knew the service, had great and long experience in thirty years' service, and the Duke was so sensible of this that when he had anything difficult or of importance to do he constantly employed him."

Sir JAMES FERGUSSON OF KILKERRAN, 2nd Baronet (1688–1759), M.P. for Sutherland 1734–35, appointed a Lord of Session 1735 and of Justiciary 1749. *Kilkerran's* " *Decisions*," a collection of the Decisions of the Court of Session, 1738–53, was published after his death, and was long a model for such compilations. He was a pioneer in agricultural reform, and the only Carrick laird to be an original member of the Society of Improvers which initiated the great eighteenth-century revolution in Scottish farming. There are three portraits of him at Kilkerran, one being by Allan Ramsay.

JAMES FERGUSON OF PITFOUR (1700–77), a great-grandson of William Ferguson of Badifurrow, elected Dean of the Faculty of Advocates in 1760, appointed a Lord of Session 1764 and of Justiciary 1765. He was noted for both his learning and his probity, and Lord Mansfield considered him " the first man at the Scottish bar." His promotion to the Bench was delayed by a suspicion of Jacobitism, for he had fearlessly defended several of the Jacobite prisoners tried for treason at Carlisle in 1746. A portrait of him by William Mosman was sold in Edinburgh in 1949.

JAMES FERGUSON (1710–76), the son of a farm labourer, born a few miles from Keith in Banffshire, astronomer and mechanic. He was largely self-taught, and with his own hands made six different orreries and an " eclipsareon "—a machine designed to show " the time, quantity, duration, and progress of solar eclipses in all parts of the earth." He lectured on astronomy and published several books on the subject, and had the unusual honour of being elected an F.R.S. without paying either the initial or annual fees. There is a pastel drawing of him in the Scottish National Portrait Gallery.

Dr. ADAM FERGUSON (1724–1816), historian and philosopher, was the youngest son of a Perthshire minister descended from the family of Dunfallandy. In early life he was an Army chaplain, and served with the Black Watch at Fontenoy. In 1759 he was appointed Professor of Natural Philosophy in the University of Edinburgh, and was one of the founders of the Poker Club to which most of the Edinburgh wits and *literati* belonged. He was the friend of almost every Scotsman of his time eminent in the worlds of art or letters. In 1764 he became Professor of Moral Philosophy, and two years later published his *Essay on Civil Society* and was made an LL.D. His *History of the Roman Republic* appeared in 1782 ; and in 1785 he resigned his Chair and took to farming in Peeblesshire. Finally he retired to St. Andrews and lived to extreme old age, a beloved and venerable figure. There is a portrait of him at the age of ninety in the University Library there, and an earlier one by Raeburn in Edinburgh University. His son, Sir Adam Ferguson of Huntly Burn, the friend of Scott, was appointed Custodier of the Regalia after their rediscovery in Edinburgh Castle.

PETER FERGUSON-TEPPER (1732–94), banker, was a grandson of Walter Ferguson, sixth and youngest son of William Ferguson of Badifurrow. His father had emigrated to Poland and there married Catherine Tepper, the sister of a Polish merchant who being childless adopted Peter as his son. Peter became a banker in Warsaw and almost the richest banker in Europe. He was created a Polish noble in 1790, and was said to be the only Protestant ever to be made a Knight of Malta. His house in Warsaw was " fitter for a king than a subject." His bank, however, failed in the political crisis through which Poland passed in 1793, the final liquidation showing a deficit of over a million ducats. He paid a visit to Scotland in 1780 when he made the acquaintance of his Badifurrow and Pitfour cousins and was given the freedom of Edinburgh.

Sir ADAM FERGUSSON OF KILKERRAN, 3rd Baronet (1733–1813), M.P. for Ayrshire 1774–80, 1781–84, and 1790–96, and for Edinburgh 1784–90, was another pioneer of agricultural improvement in Ayrshire, and a patron of science and letters, the friend of many eminent Scotsmen of his time. Burns refers admiringly to him in two of his poems. Portraits of him by Batoni, Raeburn, Andrew Plimer and George Watson are at Kilkerran.

JAMES FERGUSON OF PITFOUR (died 1820), M.P. for Banffshire 1789–90 and for Aberdeenshire 1790–1820, was the eldest son of Lord Pitfour (see above). He was an intimate friend of the younger Pitt and Dundas, and for long a familiar and popular figure in the Commons, being " Father of the House " at his death. In Aberdeenshire he was noted both as a wit and as an energetic agricultural improver.

Lt.-Col. PATRICK FERGUSON (1744–80), second son of Lord Pitfour, was a distinguished soldier who would probably have risen to the highest rank had he not been killed at the battle of King's Mountain in South Carolina, the turning-point of the American War of Independence. He is remembered as the inventor of the first breech-loading rifle used by the British Army, for which he took out a patent in 1776.

ROBERT FERGUSSON (1750–74), the poet whom Burns venerated and took as a model, was born in Edinburgh, but his father, a clerk in the British Linen Company's service, came from Tarland, Aberdeenshire. He was educated at Edinburgh, Dundee, and the University of St. Andrews, and became a clerk in Edinburgh. His poems were mostly contributed to Ruddiman's *Weekly Magazine*, and a volume of them was published in 1773. He was precocious, delicate, and highly strung, and in 1774 his mind became deranged ; he died in an asylum the same year. He is remembered not only as Burns's model but as a most vivid and racy delineator of the street and tavern life of eighteenth-century Edinburgh. A portrait probably of him is in The Scottish National Portrait Gallery.

Lt.-Gen. ARCHIBALD FERGUSSON OF DUNFALLANDY (1755–1834) served with distinction for thirty-eight years in India under the East India Company, and was severely wounded in the storming of Seringapatam. A portrait of him after Raeburn is at Dunfallandy.

Rt. Hon. ROBERT CUTLAR-FERGUSSON OF CRAIGDARROCH (1769–1838), M.P. for the Stewartry of Kirkcudbright 1826–38, was one of the earliest advocates of Parliamentary reform. He underwent a year's imprisonment on a charge of assisting the escape of a prisoner charged with high treason in 1798. He subsequently went to India where he became Attorney-General, and on his return entered Parliament. He was Judge-Advocate General under Grey and Melbourne.

Lt.-Gen. Sir RONALD CRAUFURD FERGUSON OF RAITH, G.C.B. (1773–1841), had a most distinguished career in the Army in many campaigns. The Duke of Wellington had the highest opinion of him, and, speaking of the battle of Vimiera in 1808, said that " the intrepid gallantry and conduct with which General Ferguson had led on his troops to the charge was the finest thing he had seen in his military service." The General received the thanks of the House of Commons. He was for many years a Member of it, sitting for the Kirkcaldy burghs. There is a Raeburn portrait of him at Raith, besides the well-known double portrait of him and his brother Robert as archers.

ADAM FERGUSSON OF WOODHILL (1782–1862), advocate, eldest son of Neil Fergusson of Pitcullo, advocate (died 1803), descended from the Fergussons of Bellichandy in Atholl, visited Canada in 1831, and the following year, having sold Woodhill, bought 7,000 acres of land in Western Ontario, where he built a house called Woodhill. He induced many Scottish immigrants to settle in the neighbourhood, where they founded the town of Fergus. Fergusson was a leader in agricultural development and started the first herd of pedigree Shorthorns in Upper Canada.

General JAMES FERGUSSON, G.C.B. (1787–1865), a cadet of the family of Craigdarroch, served with distinction throughout the Peninsular War, and particularly distinguished himself at the siege of Badajoz in which he was three times wounded. He was Commander-in-Chief in Malta during the Crimean War and subsequently Governor of Gibraltar.

JAMES FERGUSSON (1808–86), archaeologist and writer on architecture, was a nephew of James Fergusson of Monkwood in Carrick. His *History of Architecture in All Countries* (4 vols.), published 1862–65, was long regarded as authoritative and is by no means forgotten to-day.

Sir WILLIAM FERGUSSON OF SPITALHAUGH, LL.D., F.R.S. (1808–77), a distinguished surgeon, author of *Practical Surgery*, which appeared in 1842 and passed through many editions in Great Britain and the U.S.A. His portrait by Sir John Watson Gordon is in the Scottish National Portrait Gallery.

Sir SAMUEL FERGUSON (1810–86), the first Deputy-Keeper of the Records of Ireland, celebrated as a poet and archaeologist.

Rt. Hon. Sir JAMES FERGUSSON OF KILKERRAN, 6th Baronet, G.C.S.I., K.C.M.G., C.I.E. (1832–1907), M.P. for Ayrshire 1854–57 and 1859–68, and for North-East Manchester 1886–1906. He served with the Grenadier Guards in the Crimean War and was wounded at Inkerman. In middle life he was Governor of South Australia (1869–73), New Zealand (1873–75), and Bombay (1880–85) ; and from 1886 to 1891 he was Under-Secretary for Foreign Affairs under Lord Salisbury. After leaving Parliament he went to Jamaica on a business trip and met his death in the Kingston earthquake. There are three portraits of him at Kilkerran and another and a statue in Ayr.

Rt. Hon. RONALD CRAUFORD MUNRO-FERGUSON OF RAITH, 1st and only VISCOUNT NOVAR (1860–1934), M.P. for Ross and Cromarty 1884–85 and for Leith burghs 1886–1914, and appointed a Privy Councillor in 1910. From 1914 to 1920 he was Governor-General of Australia, in which capacity he gave much attention and assistance to the training and despatch of the Australian Expeditionary Force in the First World War. He himself considered his " best legacy " to Australia the encouragement he gave to the cultivation of its timber. He was raised to the peerage in 1920. There is a portrait of him at Raith.

General Sir CHARLES FERGUSSON OF KILKERRAN, 7th Baronet, G.C.B., G.C.M.G., M.V.O., D.S.O. (1865–1951), served in the Army for nearly forty years. He was adjutant of the 1st battalion, Grenadier Guards, 1890–94, and commanded the 3rd battalion 1904–07. From 1895 to 1903 he was attached to the Egyptian Army (of which he was Adjutant-General 1901–03), served throughout the campaigns in the Sudan of 1896–98, was severely wounded at the battle of Rosaires, and was awarded the D.S.O. In 1914 he was in command of the 5th Division, the youngest major-general in the Army List. He served throughout the First World War on the Western Front, commanding the II Corps 1915–16, and thereafter the XVII Corps. The XVII Corps held Arras in March 1918 and in August broke the Hindenburg Line at the " Drocourt-Quéant switch." Sir Charles was Military Governor of Occupied German Territory for some months after the Armistice, and retired from the Army in 1922. From 1924 to 1930 he was Governor-General of New Zealand. There are two portraits of him at Kilkerran.

Admiral Sir JAMES FERGUSSON, K.C.B., K.C.M.G. (1871–1942), second son of Sir James Fergusson of Kilkerran, 6th Baronet (see above), served with the Naval Brigade in the South African War, and commanded the Second Light Cruiser Squadron in the First World War. He was a Lord of the Admiralty 1919–20, commanded the First Light Cruiser Squadron 1920–22, and from 1924 to 1926, when he was promoted Admiral, was Commander-in-Chief of the North America and West Indies Station, retiring from the Service in 1928.

JOHN DUNCAN FERGUSSON (1874–1961), painter and sculptor, born in Leith of Perthshire crofting stock, studied in Paris and became an independent and individual artist of great distinction, associated with S. J. Peploe and other painters known as the " Scottish Colourists".

Appendix III

TARTAN

The Fergusson tartan now generally worn dates from before 1850, when it was reproduced by Thomas Smibert in his book *The Clans of the Highlands of Scotland*. Smibert depended largely on patterns which he obtained from a firm of weavers in Bannockburn.

This tartan bears a very close resemblance to the MacLaren tartan in the same collection, which differs only in having a yellow line in the sett in place of the white one ; and both are akin to the Murray tartan reproduced by James Logan in *The Scottish Gael*, published in 1831. All three therefore would seem to be native to Atholl.

Logan also recorded a tartan known as " Ferguson of Balquhidder " with a somewhat different sett of the same colours but no white line.

For the substance of this note I am indebted to Donald C. Stewart's *The Setts of the Scottish Tartans* (1950).

VARIANTS OF THE NAME

Fergusson	Ferrie	Forgie
Ferguson	Ferries	McKerras
Fergus	Ferris	
Fergie	Ferriss	
Fergushill		

THE CLAN FERGUS(S)ON SOCIETY

The Clan Fergus(s)on Society was founded in 1891. It fell into suspension at the beginning of the First World War and remained so till 1954 when it refounded with a revised constitution. The Clan Fergus(s)on Society of North America was founded in 1972. Membership is open to all who bear, have bourne, or shall assume the names of Fergusson, Ferguson, or Fegus, or any variant thereof. Further particulars and Treasurer, c/o The Scottish Tourist Board, Rutland Place, Edinburgh, 1.